Hooray for *You!*

is dedicated to

Cole James and Adam Jon whose you-ness I love.—MR

ISBN-13: 978-0-439-90824-5
ISBN-10: 0-439-90824-8

12 11 10 9 8 7 6 5 4   7 8 9 10 11/0

Printed in the U.S.A.   23

First Scholastic printing, December 2006

Illustrations by Marianne Richmond

Book design by Sara Dare Biscan

Hooray for You!

A Celebration of "You-ness"

By Marianne Richmond

SCHOLASTIC INC.

New York   Toronto   London   Auckland   Sydney
Mexico City   New Delhi   Hong Kong   Buenos Aires

For quite a long time, the world saved a place.

Millions were born, yet none filled your space...

Until the second of a minute of one special day, you took your first breath and the world said

Hooray!

Perfectly timed. Not one minute more.

You suddenly were where you were not before.

But planning preceded your earthly debut

as all was completed in the you-ness of you.

"You-ness?" you ask. Quite hard to describe,

it's your style of being, your rhythm or vibe

It's the grand sum of you that sets you apart.

Your body and brains plus your spirit and hea

"Okay..." you might think,
"but I'm not sure I see
why the big fuss
and hooray about me."

Then get set to enjoy
the big celebration
of the you-ness of you,
a remarkable creation!

Isn't it something that your wonderful face is not like another in the whole human ra

Your smile, for starters, curves up just so when you laugh and act silly or tell jokes that you know.

The body you live in
can jump, dance and play
with custom built parts
to move your own way.

Even your hair be it black, brown or red

does its own thing on top of your head.

And your certain good looks are just one teensy part
of the you-ness galore of your mind and your heart.
This is the essence of what you're about,
the true who of you within and throughout.

For instance, the way your brain likes to think.
"It just happens," you say, like a sneeze or a blink.

Automatic, for sure, but predictable not,
for no other has your process of thought.

think big ideas and original schemes. Your wide-eyed wishes are your dreamiest dreams.

And your feelings deep down are colorful creations,

a kaleidoscope of moods and emotional sensations.

Who else can know your kind of glad,

silly, excited, grumpy or sad?

There are foods you find yummy. A favorite color or two.
Things you don't like, but more that you do!

And the cool thing that's true

is how you can grow

when there's thinking to change

or new stuff to know.

You're perfect as you, but my friend, you will see
days when delighted is not what you'll be.
You might even think, "I'd sure wish to be
like him, her or them. Any person but me!"

Then stop that at once.
Put gloom on the shelf.
Say, "Good-bye doubt"
and "HOORAY SELF!"

The Big Catch

If people compare
you with another
like a mother or sister
or uncle or brother

Family Reunion

To them you can say for certain indeed,

"I'm completely for sure ME guaranteed!"

Me!

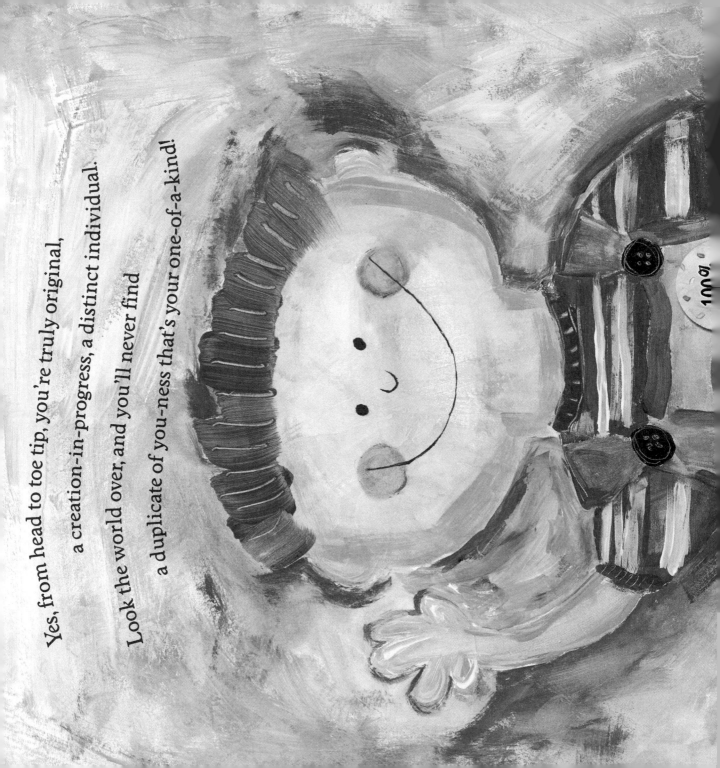

Yes, from head to toe tip, you're truly original,
a creation-in-progress, a distinct individual.

Look the world over, and you'll never find
a duplicate of you-ness that's your one-of-a-kind!

On the day you were born, the world grew by one

life with big purpose and much to be done.

Look in the mirror. Love who you see.

Stand tall. Smile big. Shout,

"Hooray for Me!"

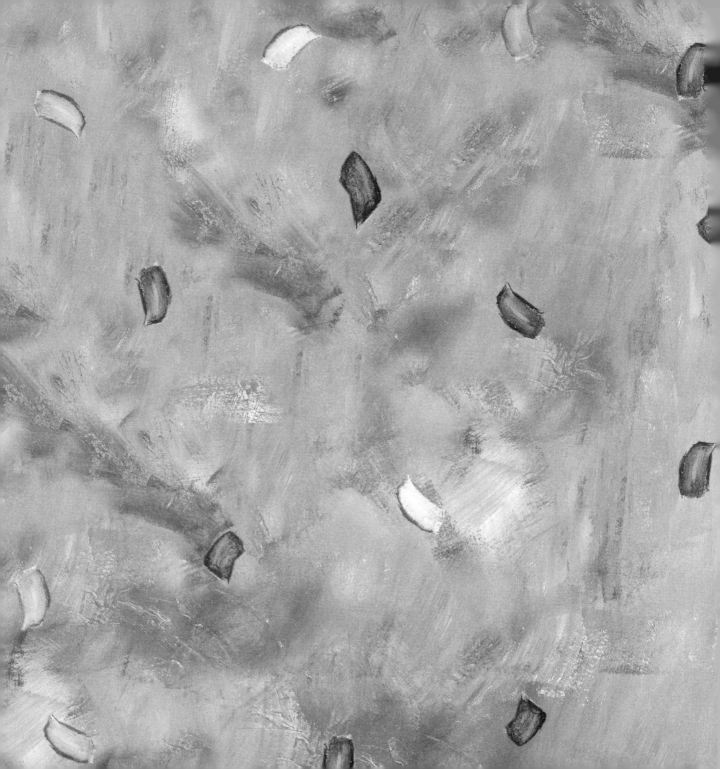

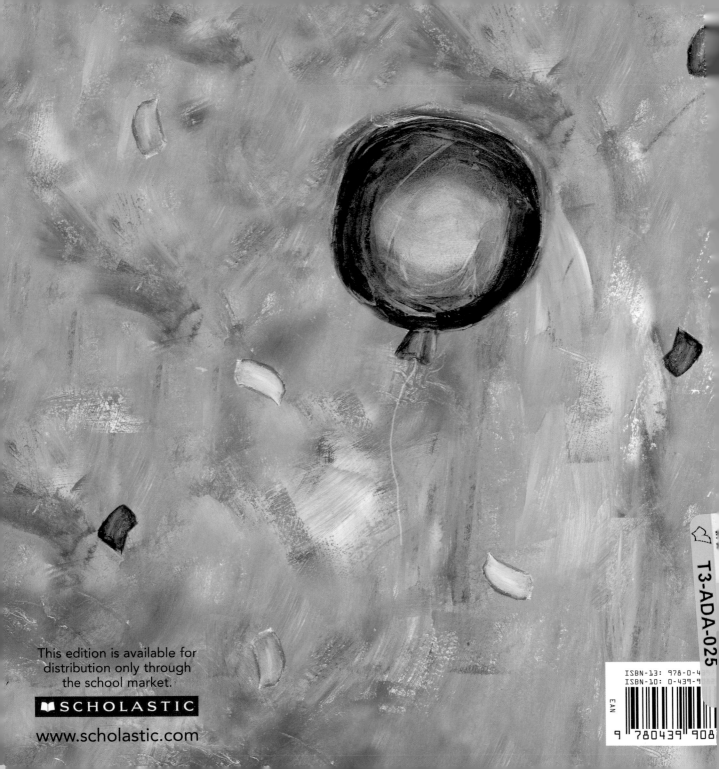

SCHOLASTIC

www.scholastic.com

ISBN-13: 978-0-4
ISBN-10: 0-439-9

EAN

9 780439 908

T3-ADA-025